Original title:
Christmas Spirit

Copyright © 2024 Creative Arts Management OÜ
All rights reserved.

Author: Aurora Sinclair
ISBN HARDBACK: 978-9916-90-842-6
ISBN PAPERBACK: 978-9916-90-843-3

Stars of Peace

Twinkling lights upon the tree,
Tinsel tangled, oh so free.
Elves in chaos, what a sight,
Cookies missing, hearts feel light.

Reindeer games, they race around,
Presents hidden, can't be found.
Mistletoe hung, a cheeky grin,
Laughter echoes, let fun begin.

A Symphony of Joy

Bells are ringing, jokes are shared,
Noisy chaos, messy hair.
Carols sung with off-key cheer,
Wink and giggle, spread good near.

Hot cocoa spills, marshmallows fly,
Grandpa's snoring, oh my my!
Stockings filled with silly things,
Laughter soars as joy it brings.

Illuminated Hearts

Glow sticks replace the candles bright,
Wacky sweaters, what a sight!
Gifts of socks, all mismatched too,
Wrap it tight, fool 'em, who knew?

Snowball fights, dodged like pros,
Funny faces, frozen toes.
Hot pies cooling on the sill,
Belly laughs, let's eat our fill.

Echoes in the Snow

Footprints squish in icy fluff,
Snowmen wearing hats too tough.
Sleds go tumbling down the hills,
Giggles soar, it gives us thrills.

Chilly cheeks and windblown hair,
Everyone's in a merry flair.
With cocoa sips and playful cheer,
Memories made, let's hold them dear.

Beneath the Winter's Embrace

Snowflakes dance with glee,
Like children on the run.
Hot cocoa spills around,
Oh, winter's so much fun!

Frosty noses twitch,
As snowballs take their flight.
We tumble with delight,
In the sparkling white.

Sledding Through Memories

On the hill we soar,
Like a rocket in the sky.
Squeals of joy abound,
As we sail, oh my!

Down we zip with speed,
Waving at the trees.
Mama's yelling loud,
"Watch out for the bees!"

The Essence of Kindness

Strangers share some cheer,
With mugs of steaming brew.
One more cookie please,
It's hard to eat just two!

A smile here, a laugh,
As gifts are passed around.
Who needs a holiday?
When joy can be found.

Laughter Wrapped in Red

In a suit so bright,
Santa trips on a toy.
Giggles fill the air,
Oh, what a silly boy!

Reindeer prance and leap,
Dancing like it's their dream.
Jingle bells are ringing,
While we're all on the team!

Beneath the Frosted Sky

Snowflakes dance like they're on a spree,
Sleds crash wildly, oh what glee!
Hot cocoa spills, what a sight,
Marshmallows fight, oh what delight!

Carols sung in a silly tone,
Neighbors laugh, they're not alone.
Elves in pajamas running about,
Spreading cheer, that's without doubt!

Whispers of the Season

Gifts wrapped up with tape gone wild,
Giggling kids, all so reviled!
Cookies burnt beyond repair,
But mom still serves, with loving flair.

Reindeer games in the front yard,
Grandpa dressed as Santa, looking hard.
A turkey dance while pies take flight,
Who knew dinner could be such a sight?

Miracles in the Air

Lights are tangled, oh what a mess,
Dad's on the roof, wearing stress.
A snowman's nose is just a stick,
But we all laugh, he looks quite slick!

Fuzzy socks on our gleeful feet,
Singing off-key, it's quite a treat.
A cat in the tree, hanging by a paw,
Along with the tinsel, oh what a claw!

The Glow of Tradition

Cousins chasing, dodging gifts galore,
Tinsel flying—oh, watch it soar!
A dog with a reindeer hat on his dome,
Chasing his tail, it feels like home.

Sipping eggnog, someone will spill,
Yet laughter echoes, a joyous thrill.
Pajamas colored in crazy hues,
This merry madness, we wouldn't refuse!

Echoes of the Past

Snowflakes dance like they know me,
Falling down on a cold cup of cocoa.
Grandma slips on her favorite mat,
Screaming 'Watch out!' like a sitcom cast.

Old ornaments stumble off the shelf,
Lands with a crash, then bounces itself.
Pictures from years when we all fit,
Now they are stretched, can we handle it?

Gathering Around the Fire

Gather 'round, the logs are stacked,
Uncle Joe's tales are somewhat whacked.
Marshmallows toast, catch on fire,
While one jumps high like it's playing liar!

Hot chocolate splashes, mugs start to slide,
The dog makes a dash, oh, what a ride!
Kids start giggling, plot to conspire,
A snowball fight quickly catches fire!

The Language of Kindness

Mittens on cats, a curious sight,
Presents wrapped in chaos and slight.
A random act – who knew it could bring,
Smiles that burst like confetti in spring?

A neighbor's pie, too spicy to try,
We laugh and we wheeze, oh my, oh my!
Yet kindness spreads like a sweet holiday cheer,
Even when cookies go missing each year!

Glimmers of Hope

The tree sits crooked, bulbs all a-scatter,
'Just like your dance moves!' someone will chatter.
As laughter echoes through the cold night air,
We toss aside worries, embrace joy with flair.

Snowmen wobble, their smiles wide,
One's wearing shades, what a goofy pride!
With each twinkling light, our hearts intertwine,
This silly season, truly divine!

A Palette of Light

The trees are decked with balls so bright,
Hiding gifts that don't feel quite right.
A cat climbs high, the star's in sight,
But ends up tangled, what a sight!

Cookies baked, a sugary mess,
Frosting faces, it's anyone's guess.
The dog steals treats, we must confess,
At least he loves us, more or less!

The Touch of Belonging

Gathered 'round in holiday cheer,
Counting down with wine or beer.
Uncle Joe tells tales we all hear,
Though each year they get worse, I fear.

Bad jokes fly like holiday cheer,
Our laughter rings, we persevere.
It's this weird flock that we hold dear,
With all our quirks, it's crystal clear!

Footprints in the Snow

Snowflakes drop and dance around,
On this white canvas, joy is found.
But wait! A slip, I hit the ground,
Laughter echoes, a silly sound!

We build a snowman with a grin,
He's got a scarf, he'll always win.
But don't ask me for help within,
I'm stuck in snow, can't even swim!

Shimmering Hearts

Lights twinkle bright, a festive glow,
But that tinsel? It's a no-show.
We've wrapped the dog in a bow,
He's now our gift, don't tell him so!

Singing loudly, off-key delight,
Even the neighbors join the fight.
The music plays into the night,
And we dance like we're in flight!

Festooned Reflections

Each bulb's a little wink, so bright,
As I juggle all my lights tonight.
Caught by the tinsel's sparkling dance,
I trip on wrapping paper—oh dear chance!

The cat climbs high, thinking it's a tree,
Swatting at baubles, full of glee.
Gifts wrapped like puzzles, taped tight in a twist,
Only to find my secret's been missed!

Hopes in the Flickering Light

A candle flickers, shadows play,
As grandma's cookies lead us astray.
We sneak a taste, just one or two,
But they vanish fast—what's a child to do?

The snowman outside looks a bit funny,
With a carrot nose that's truly sunny.
He leans a little, tipsy in cheer,
While hot cocoa spills, oh dear, oh dear!

A Season of Reflection

The tree is dressed in a tacky way,
With garlands of popcorn, oh what a spray!
Uncle Joe's apron, a sight to behold,
He's in charge of stuffing, or so he's been told.

The lights dimmed low, we share a jest,
About that sweater, it's really the best!
With laughter echoing, we raise a cheer,
For family and fun, the joy is near!

The Warmth of Old Songs

We gather 'round, voices in tune,
Singing old songs that make one swoon.
Off-key notes mix with laughter loud,
We join in the chorus, so joyful, so proud!

The radio crackles with groovy tunes,
As we dance like we're bopping on the moon.
Swap those carols for a silly song,
Laughter erupts, and we sing along!

Together by the Fire

We gather round with mugs in hand,
The warmth of laughter, oh so grand.
A cat sits perched, a sight to see,
Knocking down the tree with glee.

The cookies burn, the smoke alarms,
Yet still we laugh, and raise our arms.
Who needs a feast when snacks are fine?
We dance around with snacks and wine.

The dog has claimed the Santa hat,
He wags his tail, what's wrong with that?
We sing off-key, our voices bright,
And celebrate this jolly night.

Hearts in Harmony

The carolers came, a funny sight,
With noses red from sheer delight.
They sang a tune, but lost the beat,
A grand performance, oh so sweet.

The neighbors peek with raised eyebrows,
As we cheapen tunes with happy vows.
In mismatched sweaters, we all sway,
To rhythms that just lead us astray.

The joy is here, the spirit flows,
A dance-off starts, and on it goes!
We trip and fall, laugh 'til we cry,
And shout for joy, beneath the sky.

Threads of Hope

The presents piled, but what's inside?
Is that a sock, or gift with pride?
We guess and laugh, can't keep it straight,
Unwrapping joy, oh what a fate!

The lights are strung, but just one fell,
It flickers on, then off as well.
We fix the bulbs with duct tape flair,
Declaring it a masterpiece rare!

With every gift, we share some cheer,
Creating memories year by year.
Each laugh we share, a thread that's spun,
Together always, we are one.

The Promise of Peace

A snowball fight breaks out with glee,
A frosty blast from me to thee!
But then it snows, and we all fall,
All bundled up, we heed the call.

The cocoa spills; oh, what a mess!
We giggle hard, we can't confess.
With marshmallows flying in the air,
It's pure mayhem, but we don't care!

The stars are bright, the world aglow,
With silly tunes, we steal the show.
We promise joy and peace all night,
In laughter shared, we take flight.

Carols in the Night

In a town where socks go astray,
Olivia sings loud, come what may.
Her cat joins in, a squawking delight,
Neighbors complain, but it's quite the sight.

Snowflakes flutter, soft and bright,
Elves on rooftops take to flight.
Eggnog spills on the frosty ground,
Laughter echoes all around.

A cowbell jingles, oh such glee,
Rudolph's nose shines, can't you see?
With each off-key note that's sung,
A holiday cheer has just begun!

So gather close, don't fret the tune,
Under the glow of the silly moon.
Let's merrily sing with socks askew,
Awkward carols, all love and woo!

Ember's Embrace

A log crackles, sparks take flight,
The cat leaps up, oh what a sight!
Marshmallows melt without a fuss,
While Uncle Joe makes quite a fuss.

Kids chase snowflakes, giggles abound,
Hot cocoa spills all over the ground.
Grandma tries to bake the pie,
But it's burnt, oh me, oh my!

A reindeer hat on Grandpa's head,
He dances around, it's pure dread!
"Jingle Bells" plays at warp-speed,
Much to the neighbor's great misdeed.

In cozy chaos, joy does flow,
A fond embrace, a warm glow.
With laughter and love, the night's complete,
All wrapped up in fun, a festive treat!

The Magic of Giving

A gift appears, where could it be?
Grandma claims it's not from she.
The cat checks boxes, treats galore,
While Cousin Tim just wants to snore!

Laughter erupts with each surprise,
Uncle Bob tries to fit in ties.
A fruitcake bounces, who threw that?
Sister says, "It's just for the cat!"

The tree lights twinkle, what's the catch?
A squirrel sneaks in, who'll fetch the match?
With wrapping paper, chaos spreads,
Presents fly, oh! Who needs beds?

In this mess, fond memories rise,
The joy of giving brings the prize.
With giggles and gags, hearts will cheer,
Come gather 'round, spread some cheer!

Radiance of the Season

Twinkling lights on the house aglow,
Dad's tangled in garland, moving slow.
Mom's on the roof, yelling down tight,
"Don't touch my cookies!" - quite a fright!

The dog's in a scarf, looking absurd,
Chasing shadows, a flurry of fur.
The snowman leans, a little askew,
Waving at folks who pass, it's true!

Eggnog spills with a loud "uh-oh!"
Cousins start dancing, all to and fro.
A parade of mishaps, laughter erupts,
Just make sure the eggnog's not dupes!

So let's hold hands, both short and tall,
Embrace the joy, let merriment call.
With silly outfits and hearts that gleam,
In this season, we all live the dream!

A Time for Merriment

The snowman in the yard, so round,
With a carrot nose, the best we've found.
He's got a hat that's slightly bent,
And his stick arms show no sign of rent.

The stockings hung with mismatched glee,
Each one says 'Santa, come and see!'
But the dog thinks they're toys to chew,
And now they're full of holes – oh boo!

The reindeer games all start at eight,
But Rudolph's late, he's stuck with fate.
He's tangled up in lights again,
Told him not to play with them, amen!

The cookies burned, the milk is spilled,
Mom swears she really, really drilled.
Yet laughter fills the house so bright,
As we all fall asleep tonight.

Beneath the Boughs of Joy

Underneath the tree so wide,
A squirrel hides with nowhere to hide.
He swipes a gift, oh what a sight,
Guess he wants to join the night!

Tinsel flies like glitter bombs,
Our cat pounces, then plays with qualms.
Ornaments scatter with a clunk,
Who knew our tree's a playground trunk?

We roast the chestnuts, they explode,
And Dad just laughs, 'I can't decode!'
The fire crackles, logs start to pop,
At least our laughter will never stop!

Outside the snowflakes dance and twirl,
While Uncle Fred begins to swirl.
It's a party that never ends,
With bizarre stories from all our friends!

Ghosts of Happiness Past

The old gift wrap that's looking worn,
Contains tales of pranks that we've adorned.
Last year's sweater, bright and bold,
Looks like it came from the thrift shop gold!

A fruitcake from Auntie, what a treat,
I swear it could double as a seat.
We sliced it thin, with much debate,
Decided it would serve as bait!

But with each laugh, we share our tales,
Of mishaps, jokes, and holiday fails.
It's a blend of joy, a drink we share,
With sprightly spirits hanging in the air.

As glasses clink and cheer resounds,
We find happiness within the bounds.
Who needs the past when present's here?
A rerun laugh, that's our souvenir!

The Dance of the Evergreen

A tree that's dancing in the light,
With ornaments swinging left and right.
The star on top is kind of cocked,
It's getting ready for a frock!

The kids have strung the lights with flair,
But half of them just won't compare.
Their shining glow is hit or miss,
What's a little chaos? It's pure bliss!

The pets are tangled in the cheer,
While Grandma sings, we all won't hear.
Her voice might shatter glass and walls,
But we just laugh, no need for brawls!

So on we go, this merry band,
In winter wonder, hand in hand.
With giggles echoing through the night,
We cherish moments, what a sight!

Frosty Breath and Kindness

Snowflakes dance and swirl with glee,
Kids are sledding down the hill,
Hot cocoa spills, oh what a sight,
Laughter echoes through the night.

Scarves tied tight around all necks,
Frosty noses, no one's vexed,
Snowball fights break out in cheer,
Each friendly face brings warmth near.

Chill in the air, but hearts are bright,
Mittens lost, what a fright!
Giggles shared with every slip,
Winter's fun, a joyful trip.

As snowmen rise, just like our cheer,
Waving arms, they bring us near,
Kindness shared in every flake,
Jolly fun, for goodness' sake!

Tidings of Warmth

In cozy homes, the lights do twinkle,
Cookies baked, with hugs they sprinkle,
Grandma's tales by fire's glow,
Oh, how they make our spirits grow!

Socks not matched, but who can tell?
Laughter rises; all is well,
Dog in pajamas, what a scene,
Festive chaos, but we're a team.

Eggnog spills, but joy's retained,
Merriment cannot be contained,
Jingle bells and carols sing,
Wear your hat, let joy take wing!

Gather round for games and cheer,
Funky sweaters, let's draw near,
Tidings shared across the room,
Warmth and laughter, hearts in bloom!

Laughter Wrapped in Ribbon

Presents wrapped with bows askew,
Surprises hide, just peek and view,
Silly jokes and silly hats,
Witty rhymes and burger chats.

Cats in boxes, what a sight!
Tinsel tangles, oh what a fright,
Giggles blend with crinkling paper,
Wit unwrapped, let's bring the caper!

Tickles shared beneath the tree,
Furry friends joined in with glee,
Wrapping joy with every hug,
Laughter's warmth, it fits like a snug.

Baking fails and cupcake wars,
Flour fights and endless chores,
Memories wrapped in ribbons tight,
Mirth unfolds on this fine night!

The Glow of Generosity

Bright lights flicker, distractions few,
Giving smiles, that's what we do,
Neighbors bake, and share delight,
Friendship shines, oh what a sight!

Mismatched socks on everyone's feet,
Baking flops, but we can't be beat,
Random acts bring laughter loud,
Candlelight sways, we're feeling proud.

Stray pets find us, cuddles galore,
Wish lists tossed, we want nothing more,
Warm hearts open to all who roam,
As we share, we find a home!

Laughter brightens the darkened night,
In this time, hearts feel just right,
Generosity glows, let's raise a cheer,
For every giggle, let's spread it here!

Sleds and Joyful Hearts

Sleds are flying down the hill,
Kids are laughing, what a thrill!
Snowballs tossed, a playful fight,
We'll sled all day, then sleep at night.

Hot cocoa spills, oh what a mess,
Mom's got that look, you know the stress!
"Just one more run!" we all agree,
But our cheeks are red; we've lost the spree.

With gloves so wet, we make a friend,
A snowman's built, is this the end?
He's got a carrot, looking bold,
But really, he's just quite cold!

As night falls fast, we race inside,
With sticky fingers and silly pride.
We share our tales, the fun still gleams,
Our hearts are full, fulfilling dreams.

A Celebration of Light

Twinkling lights upon the tree,
Stringing up the joy, yippee!
Grandpa's tangled in the cords,
While grandma's perfects all the hoards.

Cookies baking, what a smell,
Some are burnt; we won't tell!
Sprinkles dance across the floor,
"More icing!" we could always score.

Neighbors gather, carolers sing,
In our hats, we're quite the bling!
Laughter echoes with each cheer,
Every moment we hold dear.

The night is filled with joy and glee,
As we sip hot punch, just a bit too free.
With cheers and giggles, we sway bright,
Who knew the dark could spark such light?

Unity Under the Stars

Snowflakes dance on winter's breeze,
Gathered under stars with ease.
Friends around, both young and old,
Tales of mischief, hilariously told.

There's Uncle Joe in his big red hat,
Wobbling over, like a clumsy cat.
With a wink and a grin, he spins a yarn,
Of sledding down the hill, now a barn!

Sipping cider, exchanging smiles,
Sharing warmth, we're here for a while.
With playful taunts to share the air,
Laughter lifts, without a care.

As the evening fades, joy lingers on,
Our hearts are light, just like a song.
We'll sing the night away, my friends,
In unity, the joy never ends!

The Warmth of Memory

Nostalgic songs fill up the air,
Grandma's cookies—oh, what a flair!
Baking fails create great delight,
"Is that a cake or a villain's fright?"

We reminisce about years gone by,
Last year's gift, oh me, oh my!
A singing fish that just won't quit,
But every giggle was truly lit!

Dad's dad jokes are still the same,
"Did you hear 'bout the reindeer names?"
We groan and chuckle, repeat the past,
This little joy seems to hold fast.

So here we toast to laughter shared,
To the little moments that truly dared.
With warm hearts we gather near,
Creating memories we hold dear.

Kindled Hearts and Joyful Souls

In the kitchen, cookies burned,
A cat swiped them, we all turned.
Laughter echoed, oh what a sight,
The oven's foe, our furry delight.

Mismatched socks upon the floor,
Grandpa drinks from the dog's old shore.
Presents wrapped in tape and cheer,
'Twas a battle 'round the tree this year!

Snowflakes fell, each one a tease,
Kids bundled up, playing freeze and squeeze.
Snowmen grinned with carrots bright,
While we all laughed at their funny sight.

Sipping cocoa with extra fluff,
This joyful chaos is more than enough.
Hearts are warm, and smiles abound,
In this merry mess, joy is found.

Serenity in the Cold

Outside it snows, a blanket white,
Inside we argue who's turn to fight.
Should we watch the game or the lights?
Oh, what a pickle, oh what a plight!

With shaky hands, the eggnog spills,
Uncle Bob's dancing gives us chills.
He says he's groovy, with flair and quake,
While the neighbors stare, for goodness' sake!

We bundled the pup, dressed him up,
In sequins and gold, our sparkly pup.
He wobbled and wiggled like a ballerina,
All for the selfies, what a diva!

Then comes the dinner, who eats what?
Veggies untouched, but pies—oh, a lot!
With laughter and plates piled high,
We feast like kings, oh my oh my!

A Whisper of Winter

Snowflakes whisper in the night,
Socks mismatched—oh, what a fright!
As carolers croon just off key,
  We try to hide behind the tree.

Mom forgot where she placed the gift,
  Wrappers crinkle, a little rift.
Kids giggle as they sneak a peek,
  What's inside? It's not for weak.

Elves in the yard, with lights so bright,
Twinkling and dancing, what a sight!
But one fell, tangled in the strings,
  Oh, what joy that laughter brings!

Snowball fights with no set rules,
Dodging and weaving like a pack of fools.
Joy spills forth, it's light as air,
  In this chaotic beauty, we share.

Twinkling Lights of Hope

Twinkling lights dance through the room,
Feeling festive, banishing gloom.
The dog thinks it's all for him,
Jumping and jiving to carol's hymn.

Grandma's cookies taste like bricks,
We laugh till our sides ache and mix.
Watering the tree with ginger ale,
Creating memories that just won't pale.

With scarves wrapped snug on every face,
Kids slide and tumble, oh what a race!
Snowmen melt, but who really cares?
This joy we savor, oh it ensnares!

As gifts are shared, what's under the wrap?
Surprises ignite like the loudest clap.
With chuckling hearts and warm repose,
Every giggle brings forth a rose.

Whispers of Snowflakes

Fluffy flakes fall, what a delight,
Landing on noses, a whimsical sight.
Snowmen with scarves, all jolly and bright,
Dancing in circles, under moonlight.

Hot cocoa spills, marshmallows explode,
Laughter erupts, as my buddy's toes glowed.
Sledding down hills, oh the journey's untold,
With crashes and giggles, the warmth can't be sold.

Frosty jokes shared, around fires we'll stand,
Stories of mischief, quite silly and grand.
Snowball fights break out, in a frosty command,
Duck, dodge, and dive, it's a snowman's land!

So let's raise a glass, to the joy that we find,
In the wonders of winter, where laughter's entwined.
With just a few friends, and a snowman designed,
We'll make merry memories, that tickle the mind!

Hearthside Harmony

Fireside crackles, oh what a noise,
Cats chase their tails, those little fur boys.
Grandma's sweet cookies, a treat to enjoy,
While Grandpa tells tales, of his childhood joys.

Socks on the mantle, filled to the brim,
But a raccoon sneaks in, and the lights start to dim.
Tinsel flutters down, as we laugh at the whim,
Chasing the shadows of a mischievous grim!

Bingo night chaos, cards mixed with cheer,
Fumbles and tumbles, like we've had too much beer.
The cat jumps and pounces, then inserts his rear,
In the potpourri bowl, oh dear, oh dear!

So let's gather round, with our funny little quips,
Share hugs and high fives, with rosy-cheeked lips.
In the hearth's glowing light, let every heart skip,
For joy is our treasure, in these lighthearted trips!

A Glimmer in the Winter Night

Twinkling lights sparkle, like stars in our sight,
Glow sticks for grown-ups, it's quite a strange rite.
Gingerbread houses, leaning left and right,
Frosting like paint, it's a whimsical fright.

The carols are sung off-key with great pride,
While pets in the corner, watch the chaos subside.
Uncle Joe's sweater, a fashion gone wide,
With reindeer and snowflakes, he'll wear it with pride.

Wrapping the presents, what a sticky mess,
Tape sticks to our fingers, it's pure puzzlement stress.
But watching the kids laughing, the heart should confess,
It's those moments like this, that we truly obsess!

So raise a glass high, to the quirks and the fun,
For every odd mishap, we laugh 'til we're done.
In this glimmering night, where our hearts all run,
We find joy in the chaos, we're a peculiar one!

The Gift of Togetherness

Gathered around, in our mismatched attire,
Sharing bad jokes, as we huddle by fire.
Aunt Sally's fruitcake, like concrete it's dire,
But we smile and nod, with unending desire.

The tree's all a-tilt, with baubles askew,
Kids argue 'bout gifts, if they're brand new or blue.
Pointing to presents, like they've found a clue,
While laughter erupts, from the coco-Roo brew.

Spilling eggnog, our favorite delight,
Dad's wearing a hat, that's a comical sight.
"Where's the nearest restroom?" he asks with fright,
While mom's busy knitting, with needles at right.

In the end, what matters, is together we cheer,
With love and sweet snacks, and a funny old deer.
For the gift that we cherish, as we gather near,
Is the joy of being odd, without worry or fear!

Festive Flurries

Snowflakes dance in the air,
And nobody seems to care.
Laughter echoes, cheeky and bright,
As we chase each other, what a sight!

Cookies stacked like towers tall,
Watch them wobble, oh they fall!
Jingle bells tied to the cat,
She pounces, oh, imagine that!

Eggnog spills, a loopy cheer,
A toast to all, raise your beer!
Friends all gather, make a mess,
Who knew joy could be like this?

Crisp and crackling, the fire roars,
Burned the ham—ah, of course!
Joy in chaos, or at least we'll try,
Festive flurries; wave goodbye!

Tinsel and Trust

Tinsel tangled in the tree,
A sparkly trap—oh, woe is me!
Ornaments dodge as we reach high,
One just shattered, my oh my!

Gift-wrap wars on the living room floor,
Scissors snipping, oh, what a chore!
Ribbons tangled like lovebirds' nests,
Mom's still searching for her vests!

Baking fails, what a sight!
Gingerbread men have taken flight!
Candy canes arm wrestle too,
It's a playful, sticky zoo!

So let's dance like no one's here,
With tinsel in our hair, we cheer!
Surrounded by laughter, warmth, and trust,
In this cozy mess, we all combust!

The Glow of Friendship

Lights are blinking, what a show!
Oh, wait, is that my toe?
Tripping over all the fun,
Laughter shines brighter than the sun!

Chili spills while we all eat,
Neighbors join; it's quite a feat!
Socks on hands, we start to clap,
Best foot forward—a slip, a snap!

Games that twist and turn the brain,
Whispers of secrets, inside jokes reign.
Do not ask me who made that stew,
We're just grateful it's not gumshoe!

Wishes float like the winter frost,
In this glow, we count what's lost.
The warmth of friendship, wild and free,
In our hearts, we can just be!

Recipes of Merriment

Add a pinch of giggles, sprinkle smiles,
Stir in some love, it goes for miles!
Knead the dough, give it a whirl,
Oops, my face—what a twirl!

Whisk away all worries and woes,
As flour flies, it gently glows.
Mix in some chaos, shake it right,
Double the fun, every bite!

Frosting fights and sprinkles galore,
This is what we all adore.
Taste the joy with every ladle,
While dancing under the kitchen table!

So gather round for a feast so bright,
Laughter, love, and pure delight.
In this recipe, we blend and stir,
Creating magic that will always blur!

Shadows of Pine and Joy

In the corner sits a tree,
Decked with lights, oh what a spree.
Cats chase ribbons, dogs play tag,
Uncle Joe's mustache starts to lag.

Eggnog spills upon the floor,
A dance-off breaks out, oh what a roar!
Grandma's cookie hat's a stunt,
And grandpa's snoring is quite the hunt.

Beneath the branches, laughter's tight,
The way we all dance, oh what a sight!
With every ornament that we hang,
Our silly songs and blissful clang.

As shadows play with joy and cheer,
We snicker at our holiday gear.
In every corner, glee will sway,
As joy and jest come out to play.

Mistletoe Moments

Under the greenery, giggles arise,
As Auntie tries to steal a surprise.
Cousin Fred thinks he's so slick,
But he's been caught—the lovey-dovey trick!

Laughter echoes with every peck,
While half the family starts to wreck.
Mom's mistletoe is a bit askew,
Yet somehow it works, even if it's glue.

Sibling rivalry's in full swing,
Who can charm with the best bling?
Amidst the chaos, love takes flight,
Stealing kisses in the moonlight.

The memories made in this silly spree,
Under the mistletoe, just you and me.
We dance and twirl with love so bold,
Making moments we'll forever hold.

Warmth Beneath the Starry Sky

Outside the glow, snowflakes dance,
As cousins slip in a daring prance.
The snowman's wearing mom's bright scarf,
While grandpa jokes, a genuine laugh.

Beside the fire, we toast marshmallows,
Each bite brings giggles, we're all heroes.
Silly stories from days gone by,
Underneath the vast, twinkling sky.

The warmth inside is hard to measure,
With laughter shared, a true treasure.
In snowball fights, the rules are bent,
But all's fair play, it's fun that's meant.

Under the stars, we find our bliss,
With goofy antics and moments we miss.
Sharing joy with family dear,
In every laugh, we spread the cheer!

The Gift of Togetherness

Wrapped in laughter, tied with glee,
The best present is you and me!
In the kitchen, a flour fight's begun,
As mom frowns, but we're still having fun.

Gifts sit quiet, but smiles are loud,
As we gather 'round, a playful crowd.
The puppy steals a wrapped-up toy,
While Dad can't find his favorite ploy.

Every moment spins me right,
In our chaos, there's pure delight.
Jokes and love fill the air,
In this warm circle, we find our share.

Togetherness shines, a beacon bright,
As we cherish each silly night.
With every chuckle and heartfelt grin,
Inside this love, we always win.

A Glimpse of Joy

In the attic, lights are strung,
A cat sits, with tinsel hung.
The fruitcake wobbles like a fish,
As uncle Fred makes one more wish.

Snowflakes dance like they're in a race,
While grandma's baking with style and grace.
The kids get wild, they jump and play,
Until the dog eats half their sleigh!

Mittens mismatched, socks all askew,
We laugh and argue on what to do.
With hot cocoa in mugs, we make merry mess,
In our holiday chaos, we surely bless!

The tree tilts like it's had too much cheer,
With ornaments falling, oh dear, oh dear!
We raise our glasses, toast to the fun,
In a world of laughter, we all are one.

Embraces and Wishes

A knock at the door, who can it be?
Oh look, it's Aunt Sally, brought cookies for free!
They crumble and scatter, it's a broken delight,
But we munch and we laugh, what a glorious sight!

The wrapping paper's a colorful mess,
As dad takes a nap, in a holiday dress.
The gifts go astray, one lands on the cat,
We giggle and wonder, "What's up with that?"

A reindeer on crutches comes into view,
"Merry everything!" shouted by our furry crew.
We dance like fools, as the music starts,
Each laugh resonates, it fills up our hearts.

So here's to the moments, both crazy and bright,
Where love and laughter take center stage right.
Holding each other through giggles and tears,
We cherish these blessings, through all of the years.

Gifts from the Heart

A sock for Dad, he's quite a sight,
Two left feet, oh what a fright!
A mug that says, "World's Best Chef",
His burnt toast skills? We all feel bereft.

A guffaw for Mom, a new pet rock,
Name it, she says, "I'll call him Doc!"
The cat now frowns, not quite impressed,
This household's circus never finds rest.

A puzzle for Sis, with pieces that flee,
"Who needs a clock when you've got glee?"
We scramble to find all the missing bits,
While our laughter dances, our patience splits.

These gifts from home, bring a chuckle wide,
Wrapped with a smile, and much love inside.

The Joy of Togetherness

Gathered 'round the wintry scene,
Fighting over the last jellybean,
A board game where no one keeps track,
Cheating's the method, no holding back!

Dad's in the kitchen, what's on the grill?
"Just a surprise!" he exclaims with thrill.
Mom's in the corner, rolling her eyes,
As smoke fills the room, it's no great surprise.

A dance party breaks, in fuzzy socks,
Flailing limbs and silly clocks.
With giggles that resonate off the walls,
We make merry chaos as laughter calls.

The fun never ends when we're close as one,
Like peas in a pod, we bask in the sun.

Celebrating with Open Arms

We wear our sweaters, light up the night,
With lights that flicker, oh what a sight!
Grandma's making cookies, a butter toast,
And no one cares about the kitchen's ghost.

Uncle Bill's joke: "What did the tree say?"
"Turn me around, it's my holiday!"
The punchline falls flat, but we still cheer,
For the warmth is humongous, with laughter near.

A tug-of-war with the last piece of pie,
Grandpa shouts, "It's me, oh me, oh my!"
We feast like kings, the table's a mess,
But the fun keeps swirling, no need to stress.

With arms open wide, we share our hearts,
In this goofy gathering, the joy never departs.

Memories Under the Twilight Sky

Beneath twinkling stars, we gather tight,
Swapping tall tales of wild snowball fights,
Mom's short on breath from the popcorn flurry,
"Who knew my stove would cause such a worry?"

A hot cocoa bar, a real grand affair,
But Dad spills all down his favorite chair.
Laughter erupts, oh, what a scene,
He laughs it off, "It's just chocolate cuisine!"

Telling ghost stories, gives us a fright,
Sister screams, "That shadow isn't right!"
The glow of the moon makes shadows long,
But our funny vibes will keep us strong.

With memories made, and hearts so light,
We dance in the twilight, oh what a night!

A Truce in the Winter

Snowflakes swirl, like my crazy hair,
Carols sung by squirrels with flair.
Mittens mismatched, but that's just fine,
Hot cocoa spills, oh sweet design!

Joyous laughter, as we slide and fall,
A snowman's hat, three sizes too small.
Frosty knows, he can't take a break,
He'll melt away if we eat that cake!

Winter wonders, each day more bright,
With cookies warmed by the firelight.
A snowball fight ensues with glee,
While grandpa snores beneath the tree!

So here's a toast, with mugs held high,
To winter fun and a pie in the sky!
Let's dance around, with silly grace,
Till we all trip over one another's face!

Beneath the Candles' Flicker

Candles twinkle, like stars gone wild,
Grandma's baking, oh, what a child!
The table's crowded, we barely fit,
And Auntie's story? A famous hit!

The turkey's burned, the ham's a flop,
But we all laugh till we just can't stop.
Bright ornaments dangle, some upside down,
As cousins wear hats like a festive crown!

Mismatched socks, we cheerfully flaunt,
'Tis the season for a goofy jaunt.
With spoons in hand, like little knights,
We duel for leftovers, oh what sights!

Beneath the glow of candles' dance,
We share weird stories, take a chance.
Life's a circus, a merry show,
With love and laughter all aglow!

Kindness in the Chaos

Shiny packages stacked to the sky,
Uncle Joe's jokes make the children cry.
The dog steals a gift and runs away,
As chaos reigns on this festive day!

Baking cookies, we made a mess,
Flour on faces? Well, that's the best!
Sprinkles flying like confetti bright,
While Grandma tests her holiday fright.

A napkin fight breaks out at the table,
And Auntie spins tales, oh so unstable.
But kindness rings, through giggles and cheer,
Despite the shenanigans, we hold dear.

Sharing smiles, we toast with cheer,
All our antics bring us near.
In the middle of this wild swirl,
Kindness shines bright, our hearts unfurl!

The Spirit of Generosity

Gifts exchanged, but lost track of who,
Someone gets socks that once belonged to Sue.
Laughter erupts as the gifts unfold,
"Oh you shouldn't have!"—said with a hold!

The cat steals ribbons, a heist in sight,
As we chase her 'round, oh what a fight!
Cookies gone missing, who took that last?
We're all on a mission, fast and steadfast.

A warm hug shared, that's the real treasure,
With jokes and jests, we find our pleasure.
Despite the chaos, we give and cheer,
In this merry mess, love's crystal clear!

So here's to sharing, in goofy delight,
With laughter and songs that feel just right.
For in every mishap, in giggles to see,
The gift of good humor is pure jubilee!

Frosty Breath and Cozy Hearts

In the chill, a breath appears,
A puffy cloud of holiday cheers.
Fingers numb, but hearts are warm,
While snowmen plot a winter charm.

With mittens lost and scarves astray,
We'll find them all, just not today!
A snowball fight, we can't resist,
As frosty flakes create a mist.

Evergreen Dreams

The tree is tall, a sight so bright,
With tinsel tangled, quite a fright!
Ornaments placed, but wait! Oh no!
That's Uncle Bob's old dancing bow!

The pine scent wafts, a fragrant tease,
While pets dream up their own mischiefs.
They'll unroll the paper with delight,
As we try to contain our laughter tonight.

Carols in the Midnight Air

Singing loud, we hit the high,
With each note, the neighbors sigh.
Oh listen close, we aren't so shy,
While off-key tunes fill the sky.

The cat looks on with judging eyes,
As we belt out our carol lies.
With some hot cocoa spilling near,
We toast to laughter and holiday cheer!

Twinkling Lights of Hope

Strung up bright, lights here and there,
One flickers on, the other doesn't care.
A tangled mess, a little fight,
Who knew the bulbs were such a plight?

The neighbors peek through curtains tight,
As we wrestle with lights late at night.
Still, we laugh 'til our bellies ache,
These moments are what we truly make!

Mirth Under Mistletoe

Under the sprig we giggle and sway,
Aiming for lips, but we kiss the bouquet.
Laughter erupts as we fumble around,
Who knew a mistletoe could leave us all brown?

The dog snags the cookies, a stealthy little thief,
Leaving us in stitches, forgetting the grief.
We dance in our socks, slipping on the floor,
After two eggnogs, we can't take much more.

A cat in a sweater, looking quite grand,
Wants to be part of this wild, crazy band.
We cheer as it pounces, our hearts filled with glee,
Celebrating the chaos of holiday spree.

As midnight chimes in, we toast our good cheer,
To awkward embraces and puns we hold dear.
With twinkling lights bursting, it's quite a delight,
Mirth under mistletoe brings laughter each night.

Echoes of Yuletide Joy

Singing off-key, we grab pots and pans,
Imagining stardom, yes, that's our grand plan.
The dog joins in too with a howl and a bark,
Creating a symphony that's quite the hallmark.

Cookies all crumbled, frosting askew,
With sprinkles that ended up stuck in my shoe.
We laugh as we bake, it's a floury disaster,
But who needs perfection when joy's the master?

The lights on the tree flicker like stars,
As we try to find snacks hidden in jars.
Unwrapping our gifts, socks only in sight,
Turns out that Santa has lost his true flight.

Echoes of laughter fill up every space,
As friends gather round with a smile on each face.
We cherish the moments, each giggle a joy,
Savoring laughter, oh, what a ploy!

Candlelight and Warmth

Candlelight flickers, it dances and shakes,
Drops of hot wax, in poetry it makes.
The cat thinks it's food, oh, what a delight,
As we chase after it late into the night.

With cocoa in hand and marshmallows hung,
We toast to the mishaps, our songs we have sung.
All cozy and wrapped in the ugliest wear,
Sweaters that shout, 'Please, have a care!'

Our hearts are aglow with stories we share,
Of past holiday faux pas that show how we care.
Each giggle a reminder that life's just a game,
In flickering candlelight, we're all rather lame.

So here's to the warmth that ignites every space,
With laughter and friendship that no one can replace.
In this winter wonderland, we all play our part,
Candlelight and warmth from the bottom of the heart.

The Magic of Giving

Oh, what a surprise, there's socks on my chair,
Cousin Joe's got a gift that smells of despair.
He wrapped it with paper from last year's dear prize,
And we all sit here giggling, can't believe our eyes.

With hands full of goodies, we nibble then pry,
Through layers of ribbons, the treasures run dry.
Who knew fruitcake could weigh like a house?
Upon tasting it, I fear my heart might rouse!

A gift card to nowhere, what fun to behold,
Yet laughter unwrapped is a heart made of gold.
As secrets come tumbling with cries of delight,
Each package is magic, even if it's slight.

The joy of the season is not what we take,
But the moments we share, and the fun that we make.
So here's to the gifts that bring laughter and cheer,
The magic of giving brings friends ever near!

Stars Over the Silent Night

Stars twinkle high, oh what a sight,
Even the snowflakes dance with delight.
Jingle bells ringing, a comical tune,
While reindeer play hopscotch under the moon.

Elves are snickering, hiding the toys,
A mix-up in colors, oh what a noise!
Santa's reindeers all tangled in lights,
Who knew prancing would cause such fights?

Hot cocoa spilling, a drip here and there,
Warm mittens giggling, they dance in the air.
The stockings are drooping, filled way too high,
Next year I'll stick with just a pie!

Under the mistletoe, a cat gives a wink,
While Grandpa's twirling, he spills his drink.
Laughter is sipped like the sweet spiced cider,
Oh, what a night—funny is brighter!

A Season for Sharing

Cookies are baking, a delightful mess,
Sprinkles go flying—oh what a stress!
The cat is now covered in frosting and fluff,
Who knew holiday baking could get so tough?

Neighbors are stopping, with pies piled high,
One's made of pumpkin, one's made of rye.
We trade funny stories, share laughs and cheer,
While Uncle Lou's snoring, we roll our eyes clear.

Wrapping that present, oh what a sight,
Presents are tangled, I'm losing the fight.
Lopsided bows and tape gone astray,
Maybe next year, I'll embrace the cliché!

In this jolly season, all mishaps are fun,
We'll laugh and we'll sing till the day is done.
So pass me that fruitcake, oh what the heck,
Who needs a holiday without a wee speck?

Unity in the Chill

Snowflakes are falling, oh what a drift,
The kids are bundled, trying to lift.
Their laughter spills out, it's a snowball war,
While I'm indoors with a snack galore.

Penguins in scarves, oh what a sight,
Sipping hot chocolate, feeling just right.
Grandma's telling tales, some funny and old,
While Grandpa is snoozing, and snoring quite bold.

Around the warm fire, we gather near,
Spinning tall tales, causing a cheer.
A sibling says something that tickles my fin,
Who knew the holidays would spark such a grin?

So let's toast together, with laughter and cheer,
Wrap up in blankets—no worries, my dear!
With fun and goodwill, we celebrate all,
In unity's warmth, may we never fall!

Fireside Whispers and Wishes

Fireside chatter, the heat makes us glow,
While marshmallows roast, it's quite the show.
A fluffy white cloud, oh wait that's my hat,
Dressed up like snowman, what a silly spat!

Tales of old Santa, with twists in the plot,
How he lost his way due to one tiny knot.
Grandma's bright stories, each one a delight,
While Uncle Fred's napping, dreaming of kite flights.

Wrapping up wishes, and whispers we share,
Does anyone know where Santa left his hair?
With laughter and joy, we'll dance through the night,
In fireside warmth, everything feels right.

Let's cherish these moments, with giggles and glee,
Creating our memories, just you and me.
For in all the chaos, we find our way back,
To each little spark—the fun we won't lack!

A Basket of Goodwill

In a basket, gifts do hide,
Reindeer snacks and fudge inside.
A cat in a hat, looking bemused,
Presents wrapped, oh so confused!

A scarf for Dad that's too bright,
And socks that glow in the night.
Uncle Joe thinks it's a prank,
But we all know, he's in the tank!

A joke book for Grandma's delight,
Her laughter echoes, pure delight.
In this chaos, joy's the rule,
Who knew goodwill could be so cool?

So gather 'round, with cheer and glee,
As we unwrap insanity.
With every laugh, a moment shared,
In our quirks, love is declared.

The Aroma of Fresh Baked Dreams

In the kitchen, chaos reigns,
Flour flies like snow on plains.
Cookies shaped like Santa's sleigh,
But they taste like gooey clay!

Mom's wearing an apron, full of dough,
The dog sits close, hoping for a show.
Baking soda, not baking powder,
Turns sweet treats into something sour!

The smell wafts through the house so sweet,
Until the timer burns our treat.
With each charred cookie, laughter grows,
We toast to our culinary woes!

With smiles wide, we munch our fail,
Fueling tales where joys prevail.
In our hearts, the warmth stays strong,
Even if the cookies are all wrong!

Radiant Smiles Across the Snow

Outside the window, snowflakes swirl,
Kids are bundled, in a whirl.
A snowman with a lopsided grin,
And funny tales where laughter wins!

Sledding down hills, cheers fill the air,
With Granny's wig up in a dare.
Hot cocoa spills on mismatched clothes,
As stories of glory come and go!

Snowball fights like epic duels,
Laughter echoes among the fools.
Inside, the fire crackles bright,
Warming hearts and toes tonight.

The joy of the season, a lovely blend,
Creating memories, time we spend.
With radiant smiles in the flurry,
We cherish these moments without worry.

Love in Every Corner

In every nook, a tale unfolds,
With silly sweaters and gifts that mold.
Tinsel hangs in disarray,
But still shines bright on this fun day!

The tree's too tall and leans to the right,
While lights blink like they're in a fight.
Cats leap up, knocking down bows,
In our home, pure joy just grows!

Chocolates hide in crafty spots,
But they're found by greedy tots.
With giggles loud and spirits high,
We celebrate the silly, oh my!

So here's to love that makes us cheer,
In every corner, far and near.
With laughter as our guiding star,
We find the warmth wherever we are!

Sweet Tidings of Comfort

Oh, the stockings are hung, but what's in them?
A lump of coal or jam from your friend.
The tree's lights blink like a disco ball,
While Grandma attempts her shortbread, oh so small.

The cookies go missing, it's quite a mess,
With crumbs on the couch, we simply confess.
The carols are sung with a quirk or two,
As the cat joins in with a mischievous mew.

A snowball fight breaks out with glee,
But Auntie slips, and oh! We all must flee.
The laughter rings out through the cold, crisp air,
As we revel in mishaps that none can compare.

So raise your glass high, let's toast to the fun,
With laughter and cheer, there's room for everyone.
For moments like these, we all can agree,
Are sweeter than chocolate or fresh-baked brie.

A Tapestry of Togetherness

Grandpa's in his chair with a blanket so snug,
While the kids play outside with a snowman hug.
The jokes fly around like confetti in air,
As we try to untangle the lights, what a scare!

Sisters bicker over which movie to pick,
While brothers are plotting their next candy trick.
Mom sighs and whispers, 'Let's keep it serene,'
But the popcorn machine is now on the scene!

The dog steals the roast right off the hot plate,
And dances away like he owns the whole state.
We chase him with laughter, it's pure joy and cheer,
As we find that the love is all that is here.

So amidst all the chaos, the laughs and the smiles,
We gather our hearts over food and the miles.
With family encircled, what else could we say?
Together we flourish, come what may.

Cradled by Snow

In a blanket of snow, we venture outside,
With mittens and scarves all tied up with pride.
The kids build a fort, it's a sight to behold,
While Dad tests the ice on the lake, brave and bold.

The snowflakes fall down like a fluffy white dream,
While we sip on hot cocoa, topped with whipped cream.
The snowball brigade launches a well-prepared strike,
And Grandma yells sternly, 'That's not how we hike!'

We slip and we slide on the ice like a show,
With giggles and tumbles, moving fast, then slow.
But moments like these, in the cold winter air,
Wrap us in warmth like a friend's gentle care.

As the moon glows above, casting shadows on snow,
Our laughter rings out, causing time to slow.
So here's to the magic, the joy it can bring,
In the frosty embrace, let your heart truly sing.

Journey Home

On a winding road, the carolers croon,
The radio crackles with holiday tune.
Dad's driving us home with a grin on his face,
While Mom's in the back, with cookies to grace.

The kids are all wondering, 'Are we almost there?'
While plotting to sneak in a bite of the air.
The miles roll on by, filled with laughter and cheer,
As we sing off key, nobody seems to care.

With a pothole or two and a wrong turn as well,
We cheerfully jive through our own little hell.
But the joy in our hearts keeps our spirits aglow,
As we pull up to home, where warmth is the show.

So raise up a toast to our journey so sweet,
For no matter the bumps, it's our love that can't beat.
With lights all aglow and the scent of delight,
We gather together, all feeling just right.

Crystals of Laughter

Jingle bells ring, oh what a sound,
As snowflakes fall softly to the ground.
Grandma's baking cookies with extra zest,
Who knew a burnt batch could be such a jest?

Reindeer are flying, or so they say,
But they're just lost in a game of play.
Santa's new sleigh has a mind of its own,
It took a detour—now where has he flown?

Elves in the workshop are snickering loud,
Making odd toys that they're proud to endow.
Dancing around with mismatched socks,
Wrapping up gifts in bitter old box!

So raise up your mugs, let's toast to the cheer,
For even the grinch finds some joy this year.
Laughter is golden, just look and you'll see,
The magic is here, let's all just be free!

Candlelit Wishes

Candles are flickering, shadows do dance,
A cat's made a mess—it's all of his plans.
He's tangled in garlands, just look at his plight,
As we giggle at his festive, furry delight.

Wishes are whispered, as starlight behaves,
But don't trust the glow of those candlelit waves.
Uncle Joe's face, covered in whipped cream,
Brought laughter alive like a silly daydream.

Eggnog spills over—what a sight to behold,
The secrets of cheer, in laughter retold.
With each clink of glasses, the humor will rise,
As we laugh 'til we cry, under twinkling skies.

Let's count every chuckle, each snort and each grin,
As moments of joy wrap us warmly within.
The light may flicker, but fun's here to stay,
Behind each bright wish lies a giggle at play!

The Promise of Tomorrow

Tomorrow brings visions of ribbons and cheer,
But tonight we're tangled in last-minute fear.
With lists and with jingle bells jingling so loud,
We're all stressing out, oh isn't it proud?

We'll wake up to presents, or maybe it's snow,
Hopes stacked like gifts, but we still don't know.
The dog ate the wrapping, the cat batted a tree,
And Uncle Tim's hiccups make quite the decree!

Magic is brewing in pots full of stew,
But watch out for spills, it's all fresh and new.
We'll gather together, our hearts all aglow,
Yet slip on a toy, and see how we go!

So here's to tomorrow, with laughter in hand,
For every small blunder creates a grand stand.
With chuckles and warmth, we'll dance through the night,

In the comfort of love, everything's alright!

Frosted Dreams

Frosted the window, a scene oh so bright,
Snowmen are winking, a comical sight.
They've hats from the closet, mismatched above,
Dancing in snowflakes, like giggles of love.

The children are giggling, all bundled up tight,
Until they fall down, what a wonderful fright!
Their sleds are now flying, or maybe they're not,
The speed of their laughter ends up being caught.

Grandpa's on ice skates, looks more like a frog,
His twirls are a miracle, but oh, what a slog!
"Watch how I glide!" Oh, what a sweet dream,
Then lands on his back, with ice cream to beam!

So gather around for these frosted delights,
With smiles and with jokes, through long winter nights.
The magic of fun lies in warmth of our smiles,
As laughter entwines us, through all of the miles!

Milton Keynes UK
Ingram Content Group UK Ltd.
UKHW020735301124
451807UK00019B/792

9 789916 908433